The Anxious Preoccupied Attachment Style Workbook

A Guide for the Anxiously Attached to Heal and Start the Journey Toward Becoming Secure

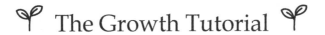 The Growth Tutorial

Disclaimer

The information within this book is meant to provide insight and education for individuals. It should not be used to replace any form of therapy or counseling and is not intended to do so. It is recommended that anyone with emotional or mental distress contact professional services. Though every effort has been made to confirm the accuracy of the information by thorough research, the author and publisher are not held responsible for errors or liability with use of this book whether directly or indirectly. The material and tools used within this book include research from other parties and they hold ownership of their ideas. The guidance given in this book may have different results for each individual and is not to be a substitute for treatment of any kind.

Table of Contents

Introduction

Hello, there. Welcome to your guide, whether it is to heal your own attachment style, understand someone else's, or to simply learn more about attachment theory.

In the beginning of this book, some of the information may be eye opening or basic depending on your prior knowledge of attachment styles. As we move further together, we will dive into more in depth material and exercises.

This book includes data and tools from many resources, including academic, and learned ideas over time. Sharing these concepts and practices with you will help you truly understand what attachment theory is, what each style means for you or a loved one, and guide you into healthy activities and thought patterns while reprogramming the negative ones that bring unnecessary pain and suffering into your life.

Though you may have an anxious or avoidant attachment style, or mix of both, there is hope to become secure. It is possible to leave behind the self-destructive patterns and have a brighter outlook on life. Though it may be cliché, there is light at the end of the tunnel, and you are about to see it.

The information given at the beginning of the book is to give you an understanding of attachment styles so you can better comprehend our lesson in this book about the anxious preoccupied attachment style. In having background knowledge, you will come to know more about why you (or your loved one(s)) have certain behaviors, patterns, thoughts, and fears. You will be better able to grasp the workbook exercises and the material that comes with them. Reading the prior information we are about to get to is also a great way to review. However, if you already have a strong understanding of attachment theory and what it entails, feel free to skip ahead – there is a table of contents page just before this section that can help you find your place.

Congratulations on taking this exciting step.

What You Will Learn

- What attachment theory really is, its history, and why it is important
- How attachment styles are formed
- What the four attachment styles are with examples of each
- How the anxious attachment style interacts with other styles and its own
- The anxious attachment style's common protest behaviors and triggers
- Core wounds, the six human needs, love languages, the classifications of boundaries, and the main areas of life
- 22 exercises to heal the self, overcome unnecessary suffering, including codependency and the strong fear of abandonment, and strengthen relationships with reprogramming

Chapter 1: A Brief Overview of Attachment Styles

What is Attachment Theory?

Attachment theory is a psychological framework developed in the 1950s by British psychologist John Bowlby and expanded on by American-Canadian psychologist Mary Ainsworth, and later, others. Bowlby sought to understand the emotional bonds and relationships between individuals, focusing on infants with their primary caregivers. This theory suggests that infants are biologically predisposed to form certain attachment styles in order to survive and receive care. Due to each individual infant's upbringing and environment, an attachment style will be formed, having a strong influence on the social, emotional, and cognitive development of the child through life.

The Strange Situation Experiment was conducted and later published in 1969 by Mary Ainsworth. She developed a test involving an infant's behavior with their mother leaving a room and a stranger entering the same room. There were several steps to this experiment that led to more understanding of attachment styles. The child's willingness to explore, their behavior upon their mother returning, and their level of anxiety toward being separated from their mother and being alone with the stranger were all factors in determining the infant's attachment style.

In the case that the child is held by the mother upon her return and calms down, then feels comfortable enough to play with the toys in the room, the **secure attachment style** is shown. When the mother comes back and holds her infant yet is ignored, the child avoiding eye contact and becoming tense, shows the **avoidant attachment style**. This style also showed the least amount of distress when the mother left the room. If the mother comes back, holds the infant, yet the infant keeps crying and wants nothing to do with the toys but continues to cling to the mother, this child shows **anxious attachment style**.

The **disorganized attachment style** was later discovered in 1986 by Mary Main and Judith Solomon. When they did the same experiment, they found contradictory behaviors taking place in the infant, including fear, freezing, and strange movements. At times, the infant would run toward the mother, then run away.

There is only one secure attachment style, which simply enough is called secure attachment. The three insecure attachment styles are dismissive avoidant attachment (also known as avoidant), anxious attachment (also known as anxious preoccupied or anxious ambivalent), and disorganized attachment (also known as fearful avoidant or anxious avoidant).

A Breakdown of Each Style

Secure:

Those with a secure attachment style are confident in their caregiver's ability and responsiveness. They feel comfortable to go out and explore the world, trusting that their caregiver will be there when they return. They know when they need support and comfort, their caregiver will provide that for them. This results in a more positive mindset, growing trusting and loving connections with others.

This is why in the experiment, the securely attached infant calms as soon as the mother returns. The caregiver is a place of comfort and the infant sees no reason to feel burdened any more.

Securely attached individuals feel seen, understood, and valued from a young age. During early stages of life, they also felt safe and as though they could comfortably ask for reassurance and validation without any form of punishment. As they grow, they are able to find a balance between relying on others as well as meeting their own needs. This allows them to feel comfortable showing vulnerability while still being interdependent.

Most of the time, those with a secure attachment style have it because of the way they were brought up and the relationship they had with their early caregivers and environment. In other cases, the secure attachment style is learned after having an insecure attachment style, using tools (as we will use soon in this book). Securely attached individuals tend to have a positive outlook on themselves and others, leading to confidence, openness, a better sense of peace. They do have negative experiences, just as anyone has, however, they are able to assess the situation in real time, being able to separate people from certain actions.

Quick Signs:

- Knows how to set healthy boundaries
- Easier to trust others
- High-self esteem
- Able to self-reflect, even in relationships
- Easier to connect with others
- Able to regulate emotions quicker
- Knows own needs and able to meet them
- Comfortable whether alone or in a relationship
- Feels comfortable asking for help
- Communicates well and able to navigate conflict
- Respects personal values

- Specifically in a romantic relationship: Great communicator, including sharing vulnerably; trusting, respectful of both their and their partner's boundaries and needs, warm, understanding of partner's interests outside of relationship, calm and attentive when in conflict, enjoys time with partner while saving time for individuality

Anxious:

People who are anxiously attached can feel intense anxiety in relationships (platonic and romantic). They tend to become preoccupied with the availability of those they are attached to, leading to high levels of emotion, constantly fearing abandonment. They can be seen as clingy, and have difficulty with rejection and self-esteem.

During the experiment, the anxiously attached infant would not stop crying because of the immense fear and uncertainty felt by the mother leaving.

Anxiously attached individuals may have had caregivers that were inconsistent, those that could be attentive sometimes, but were seemingly detached at other times. Some caregivers may have been overwhelmed or even unintentionally made the child feel responsible for the caregiver's feelings. The mixed signals leave the child confused and unable to know what type of response will be given by the caregiver(s) in the future. This leads to the child interpreting that their needs may or may not get met. In some cases, a caregiver may appear overbearing in a way to get their own needs met from their child, many times not even realizing this. At times, this type of parenting may be a result of the caregiver being raised a similar way and having anxious attachment themselves.

Those with this attachment style crave intimacy with the constant fear that it will leave when they do find it. Being alone increases this fear. Since they have low self-worth and a high opinion of others, they tend to gain acceptance through others, feeling the need for outward approval. When they are in a close relationship, they constantly seek to be closer, fearing that any change or distance will result in being abandoned. This can come off as clingy to those close to the anxious individual, and will most times have the opposite effect, pushing others away. It is a continuous cycle for the anxiously attached, feeling safe for a short period of time, and then fearing abandonment again just as soon. It is a rollercoaster of emotions with the highs feeling grandiose and the lows very strengthened as well.

Quick Signs:

- Fears of rejection, abandonment, being alone
- Feeling unworthy of love
- Low self-esteem
- High sensitivity
- Constant need for approval and reassurance
- Difficulty with boundaries
- Difficulty trusting others
- People pleasing and codependency
- Overanalyzing and very intuitive
- Craving intimacy and constant availability from another person

<u>Dismissive Avoidant:</u>

Dismissive avoidants tend to appear emotionally distant and highly independent. They suppress their needs and emotions and are not usually very vulnerable. When it comes to finding a partner, this attachment style may have difficulty opening up, feeling it is safer to avoid strong emotions and spend plenty of time alone. They can end up feeling overwhelmed by relationships and self-sabotage when there is a sense of commitment due to fear of intimacy.

In the experiment, the dismissive avoidant infant becomes closed off to the mother, feeling as though their needs will not get met even if they try to convey them, and feeling safer if they avoid rather than express their feelings.

Growing up, the dismissive avoidant may have had a caregiver that was neglectful or emotionally distant, leaving the child to basically fend for his or herself. The caregiver(s) may have expected independence from their child or rejected the child when expressing emotions, not meeting the child's needs. This teaches the child to be completely self-reliant, leaving the child with the sense that others cannot be relied on.

The dismissive avoidant will place autonomy above emotional intimacy and connection, viewing any type of vulnerability as unsafe since they did not feel safe going to their caregiver with openness. They can come off as extremely confident, but underneath is a sense that they are unworthy of love. Even though they hide the need, and sometimes are not quite aware themselves, there is a hidden fear of abandonment, believing that when someone sees them for who they think they are, they will be left, and so this attachment style tends to leave teetering relationships first so they will not feel that pain of abandonment. They also have a tendency to shut down instead of partaking in conflict as this feels too vulnerable for them. (Ways to communicate in a healthy and safe way will be taught later in this book).

Quick Signs:

- Feel safer alone
- Difficulty trusting others
- Very independent
- Avoid intimacy and vulnerability
- Difficulty to commit
- Uncomfortable expressing needs
- Underlying sense of being defective or thinking there is something wrong with them
- Highly sensitive to rejection
- Deep fear of abandonment

Disorganized:

This attachment style can be seen as a mix between the anxious style and the dismissive avoidant style. You can think of a spectrum with one of these two styles on either side. Someone who is fearful avoidant may show more signs of being dismissive, or more signs of being anxiously attached. This can even change depending on who they are around. If someone who has the disorganized attachment style is involved with someone who is a dismissive avoidant, they may sway more anxious. Whereas if the same person is involved with someone who is an anxious-preoccupied, more signs of their dismissive side will most likely be triggered. They can be hot and cold toward those in their life and be untrusting of their partners, experiencing jealousy due to fearing betrayal right around the corner.

In childhood, the disorganized individual may have had some sort of trauma early on. This could be neglect, abuse, or some reason to fear their caregiver. Or there may have been other types of trauma where they felt their safety was at risk – early divorce, loss of a parent (though these can trigger other attachment styles as well). Other causes leading to this style could be if something of heavy weight happened that broke the child's trust, if the caregiver became emotionally needy, threatening language was used often, or the caregiver also had this attachment. Inconsistent parenting shows up here, too. They perceive their caregiver(s) as unpredictable, unsure if they can feel safe in their environment and whether they can feel comforted by the caregiver since sometimes they do and other times they do not.

The disorganized individual craves closeness like the anxious, yet fears it as the dismissive does. They tend to have a negative outlook on themselves as well as others. There is this strong desire to become close, but once they do, there are conflicting emotions, making them want to distance, while at the same time, wanting more closeness. This is because though they deeply want that intimacy, they have a hard time trusting people and fear opening up. Believing they'll end up being rejected, disorganized individuals have a cycle of their own, searching for connection, and then becoming afraid of the closeness and self-sabotaging. What makes them feel safe is also what they fear.

Quick Signs:

- Hypervigilance
- Difficulty trusting
- Unable to regulate emotions well
- Poor boundaries
- No sense of safety
- Behaviors to gain control in order to feel safe

- Contradictory behaviors
- Jealousy and fear of betrayal
- Hot and cold
- Clingy in one instance, yet distant in another
- Signs of the anxious and avoidant styles

Interactions Between Anxious Preoccupied and Other Attachment Styles

While attachment triggers tend to be more prevalent and stronger in romantic relationships, it is important to note that they also will show up in familial relationships, friends and other platonic relationships, including in the workplace. And though one attachment style shows up with a partner, a different one can show up with a friend. It is common for someone to have traits of more than one attachment style while still having a dominant style.

Anxious Attachment & Secure Attachment

In the beginning, the anxious will feel comfortable in this dynamic because they will feel seen and heard, accepted and wanted. The secure will admire the love they receive from the anxious preoccupied. Even though one person is secure, the anxious will cling and become needy. They may reach out for more control in an attempt to keep the secure person close in fear they may leave if given the chance. This will not trigger a secure individual as it would a disorganized or dismissive, but the secure may still feel overwhelmed and need to take time on their own to hold their boundaries to self. The anxious will bring out their people pleasing tendencies, self-sacrificing to hold their position in the secure person's life – something they think they must do to be worthy. This can lead to resentment if they feel they are giving too much, not listening to their own boundaries and needs.

With the secure person's patience, healing from the anxious, and communication, this can be a much better relationship.

Anxious Attachment & Anxious Attachment

A relationship between two anxiously attached individuals will boast high levels of connection. Each may be ready to listen to the other and give what they expect the other person needs. However, there are also high levels of anxiety. By giving, and usually not communicating well, they both may begin to feel taken advantage of or as if the other is not giving them what they *really* need. This will breed resentment. And though they are both giving to the other, it is partly done out of trying to keep the other from abandoning them, and it will feel like they are sacrificing for the good of the relationship.

Anxious Attachment & Dismissive Avoidant Attachment

Like in their childhood, anxiously attached individuals are familiar with inconsistency, which happens in this dynamic. The dismissive will feel love from the anxious, making them feel supported and safe, and they will see positive traits in them that they repress. The anxious will also see traits and qualities in the dismissive that they repress.

The anxious will people please and become confused when the dismissive doesn't show love in the same ways they do, leading them to believe at times it may not be there, perceiving things how they feel instead of how things are.

As the dismissive takes the space they need, the anxious will cling desperately trying to close that space as they feel rejected. This will cause the dismissive to withdraw more.

Activating strategies occur for the anxious, while deactivating strategies occur for the dismissive here. The anxious may even threaten to leave, not to really leave, but in hopes to get a reaction from the dismissive avoidant that *proves* they care – this strategy is actually harmful to both parties.

This duo tends to get caught in the *anxious-avoidant trap*, which is a cycle of pushing and pulling. Each time the dismissive pulls back, the anxious panics thinking the dismissive is leaving, and clings more, while the dismissive fears their need for space is in danger and pulls away more.

Anxious Attachment & Disorganized Attachment

This relationship may seem like it is meant to be in its first stages. But throughout, it is a rollercoaster filled with many highs and lows for both parties. They both will feel a strong connection and passion, and share an infatuation with each other. Their needs will feel met and they will be on the same page for a while. Once the disorganized individual begins to open up more to the point they feel too seen, they will shut down or distance in an attempt to feel safe. The anxiously attached will take this personally, feeling as though they are about to be abandoned and are unwanted. This will trigger the anxious person to regain closeness as they are experiencing mixed signals like from when they were a child. The anxious individual may begin clinging, thinking this will keep the disorganized from leaving. However, this pushes the disorganized person to feel smothered and to react in the opposite way, perhaps distancing more or becoming volatile. Then the disorganized will come back after feelings of guilt become too heavy, and the two will reconcile.

The disorganized being with an anxious will likely bring out more traits of the dismissive, causing the disorganized to seek distance more often than seeking intimacy. Deep closeness is common for this pairing, though arguments and the cycle of clinging, withdrawing, and returning are as well.

Chapter 2: A Deeper Dive into Anxious Attachment

When the anxious-preoccupied attachment style is not understood by the person identifying with it, or the people around them, just like other insecure attachment styles, it can be difficult. The anxiously attached person unknowingly gives into fear, using activating strategies to reduce pain. The people in their lives many times misunderstand their actions. Learning more about anxious attachment is important as is putting in the effort to work on it in order to become secure! There are mountains of valuable information on this attachment style and others, but to be concise, we will visit a few more interesting points on the anxious-preoccupied attachment style before getting to the tools you can use in your journey becoming more secure.

Common Triggers of the Anxious Attachment Style

Feeling unappreciated or unwanted:
Anxiously attached individuals put a lot of time, effort, and energy into the people they care about. They have low self-esteem already, so when they try in any type of relationship and perceive they are not wanted or do not get appreciation, this can feed the fear and negative feelings in them.

Distancing:
Especially when done without direct communication, or suddenly, or something out of routine, this can be very painful and frightening to the anxious-preoccupied. They can attribute space to losing interest, them being unwanted, not good enough, or unimportant, that someone "better" is replacing them, abandonment is in sight. Unless there really are troubles in a relationship, which may need its own discussion, anxiously attached individuals need specific reasoning for distance, or may otherwise formulate their own negative stories.

Being dismissed or undervalued:

The anxious-preoccupied craves connection, which allows them to feel safe in a relationship. When they feel as though they are being dismissed, it will feel as though there is a lack of connection. If there is no or little communication, they will fill in the blanks to find a reason for why they are being dismissed, usually a negative and hurtful one. They already feel less than, so when something happens that makes them feel they are not enough, even only perceived this way, they will believe it.

Rejection:

This could range from an ignored text to a breakup. Anxiously attached individuals feel the need for others to validate them, finding their worth in other people. By being rejected, even if it is not a personal attack, the anxious-preoccupied will take it this way, and it can be very painful as they begin to tell stories about why they are being rejected.

Abandonment:

Whether being left, the fear of imminent abandonment, or feeling lonely, this is a big fear for the anxious preoccupied. This comes from the incongruency during childhood while feeling abandoned either physically or mentally by a caregiver. This individual lacks a relationship to self, meaning they do not usually know how to be alone. They strive for connection with others and are usually in tune to the needs of others, people pleasing in an attempt to keep those connections, but they do not tend to understand or meet their own needs.

An argument, a change in routine, or perceived distance can create fear in the anxious individual, causing them to cling as they panic that they will be left.

Common Protest Behaviors or Coping Mechanisms of the Anxious Attachment Style

Giving excessively:

This can be with materialistic things or giving time or effort. Though giving can be a wonderful display of love and affection, it can become unhealthy when done for the wrong reasons. One of these reasons is to win someone over by giving excessively. The anxious attachment style tends to give past the point of ignoring their own needs and crossing their own boundaries in hopes to keep someone else around or content. However, this can backfire in more ways than one. Not only is the anxiously attached individual ignoring their needs, but they may also grow resentment the more they cross their boundaries, feeling as though the people they're giving to are taking advantage of them or not giving back as much. They keep giving, though, afraid that if they do not or if they say *no*, they will lose or upset the other person – something that stings this attachment style since they get much of their worth through others.

Becoming critical:

During an argument or while expressing hurt feelings, the anxious-preoccupied may lash out, saying critical and sometimes hurtful things. The intention is not to cause the other person pain, but to get heard. When an anxiously attached individual does not know how to communicate in a healthy way, the critical words are their way at trying to communicate in the best way they know.

Testing people:

This can happen when an anxious-preoccupied wants to check how much someone cares. They may put someone in a situation or ask them things they already know the answer to in order to find out whether this person is trustworthy. They also push people away in hopes they will return, *proving* they do care and creating validation.

Attempting to create jealousy:

This is an attempt to recreate connection, validation, certainty, love, and care. The anxious-preoccupied wants to know they are important and wants to see their partner or friend react with jealousy, figuring if they do, they must care a lot about them. Sometimes, doing this can create the desired outcome, while other times, specifically when done toward a dismissive or dismissing-leaning disorganized, it can backfire, getting pushed away instead of pulled closer. Either way, it is an unhealthy behavior that is trying to get an unmet need met. So, it is important to find better ways to meet those needs and to communicate with the person instead of creating jealousy.

Constantly checking in on another person:

When there is distance, the anxious preoccupied becomes more anxious, triggering their coping mechanisms, making them want to decrease the space. They may call or text a lot, especially when their attempts are not getting answered when they expect them to. They may get on social media to check on someone's activity or ask about them to friends and family. They may try showing up where they know the other person is. This is even more common when there is an argument, projecting from their own perspective that the other person would love for them to reach out in these ways since that would make *them* feel loved. This is a cry for connection, and a hint that more time with self is needed to be nurtured.

Chapter 3: Guides

These guides will help us with the workbook exercises in the next chapter. You are encouraged to come back to review and further understand these following sections and definitions.

The Six Human Needs

Tony Robbins framed this model. The way people meet or ignore these needs is a large factor in determining how someone lives life and the experience they have. Each person ranks these differently based on their own personality, but they are all important, and when one is left out, there in an imbalance felt.

Certainty:
This is the need for safety, security, protection, comfort, stability, and predictability.

Uncertainty:
This is the need for change, excitement, novelty, freedom, and exploration.

Significance:
This is the need to feel important, needed, to matter and have meaning, have some sort of positive status.

Love and Connection:
This is the need for mutual love, closeness, to connect with someone.

Growth:
This is the need to grow, learn, develop, strive for something important.

Contribution:
This is the need to give, help, provide service to others.

The Five Love Languages

From Gary Chapman, the five love languages. Though everyone may enjoy all five of these ways to show love, there usually are a top one or two. People give and receive love in different ways, and one person's way to show affection will be different from another. These are ways we show love to everyone in our lives. For couples, it is important to find out and communicate what your own love language is and that of your partner.

Words of Affirmation:
Feeling loved by someone vocalizing what you mean to them. Receiving words of praise and positive remarks. Feeling appreciated and accepted and important when hearing these. Things as seemingly simple as *thank you for paying for dinner, that was really thoughtful* or *you sounded great at your presentation today* will go a long way, especially for someone with this as a top love language.

Quality Time:
Feeling loved by spending time with someone. Keep in mind the keyword here – quality. Two people sitting in the same room while one person is on their phone the whole time and the other is doing homework will not feel like this is fulfilled. Quality time is enjoying each other's company, partaking in the same event, talking with one another, playing a game together. Spending two hours of quality time will make someone feel more loved than five hours of distracted time.

Acts of Service:

Feeling loved by someone putting in the effort to help them or doing something kind and thoughtful for them. This can make someone feel like they have a teammate and they have someone who cares about them and thinks about them. Helping them with a project like yardwork, building a shelf, cooking dinner, even accompanying them to run errands. Note here that this is mostly valued when it's offered instead of being asked.

Gifts:

Feeling loved by receiving gifts. This does not mean they want to be showered with jewelry and cars or care about the monetary value of a gift. Here, it really is the thought that counts. They appreciate the time put into picking something out and that they were on your mind. It could be surprising them with the hat they've been wanting, or dropping their favorite lunch off at work, or as small as picking them a flower.

Physical Touch:

Feeling loved by being shown physical affection. This does not have to mean sexually. It can be holding hands, hugging, cuddling, having some sort of physical contact. For those that prioritize this, it can boost emotional connection, helping with trust and vulnerability.

The Six Classifications of Boundaries

Being able to understand how these affect each of us personally and knowing when we feel comfortable or like lines are being crossed can greatly help us protect ourselves.

Time Boundaries:

Ask, how much time do I feel comfortable, or can I afford, to give here?

Intellectual Boundaries:
Ask, how will I respond to others not respecting my ideas?

Material Boundaries:
Ask, what am I able to share?

Physical Boundaries:
Ask, who and what am I comfortable being around, and what do I deem an appropriate way for someone to touch me?

Sexual Boundaries:
Ask, what am I comfortable with sexually?

Emotional Boundaries:
Ask, what do I feel comfortable communicating and how much am I able to hear emotionally from others right now?

Core Wounds List

A core wound is usually formed in childhood and carried, sometimes, throughout life, but by reprogramming these beliefs, can be worked through. These are ideas that we subconsciously repeat and feel a deep emotion to. They give us a sense of insecurity and highly influence how we think and what we believe about ourselves. Below you will find a list of core wounds, generated by Thais Gibson.

I am abandoned	*I am unsafe*	*I am unloved*
I am unworthy	*I am defective*	*I am excluded*
I am not enough	*I am weak*	*I am rejected*
I am disrespected	*I am helpless*	*I am bad*
I am misunderstood	*I am disconnected*	*I am disliked*
I am stupid	*I am unimportant*	*I am unheard*
I am trapped	*I don't belong*	*I am powerless*

Areas of Life

These are the areas in which we spend our lives. We decide how much effort to put into each one and may be better at respecting some more than others, but at the end of the day, we need to nourish each area for a better quality of life.

Career:

What we want for our job, goals, and dreams. How we want to earn income.

Financial:

How we spend our money. Saving tactics. Paying off debts. Investing and budgeting.

Spiritual:

Practicing gratitude and forgiveness. Relationship with God. How time is used for prayer and deepening connection.

Emotional:

Being able to regulate emotions. Understanding and listening to what your emotions are communicating.

Mental:

Learning a skill. Developing yourself and your knowledge.

Physical:

How you treat your body. Exercise and diet. Sleeping and moving.

Environmental:

Keeping your environment organized, and on a larger scale, taking care of the planet.

Relationships:

Relationship to self, partner, family, friends, community. Effort given to socializing or taking care of yourself.

Chapter 4: Exercises

The following pages will include exercises that will deepen your understanding of yourself, your – or someone else's – attachment style, and many common factors that cause insecurities in people. It is important to really take your time with these and do them fully as the more effort you put in, the more you will get out of it. You may find that doing some of these more than once is a greater help and that you may uncover more about yourself the more you do specific exercises.

Be gentle and patient with yourself. Certain exercises may be more difficult than others. Remember, these are not meant to be a substitute for therapy or any type of counseling. Though you will find better ways to communicate, understand yourself and the people in your life, if there is abuse in a relationship, it is never acceptable, and you are encouraged to get out and find professional resources to help you.

Feel free to do these exercises in any order and to use the previous material, including the guides to ensure your understanding and help you best complete the worksheets to begin reprogramming your insecurities.

Exercise 1: Core Wounds and Reprogramming Your Core Beliefs

In childhood, you may have experienced trauma around specific core wounds. For instance, if you had a caregiver that would rarely listen to you, respect your needs, or ask your opinion, you may feel unheard. As you go through life, you will carry this belief with you, feeling as though no one takes your thoughts and ideas into consideration. This will leave you with an insecurity, making you believe you will be unheard even before you try. You will figure no one wants to hear you, so why bother.

If you're having doubts, yes, your negative beliefs *can* be changed. When we are born, the only fears we have are falling and loud noises. The rest of our fears are learned. This means, if these core beliefs have been programmed into us, we have the ability to reprogram them.

To reprogram your core wounds, you need to know what they are, and then teach yourself to believe the opposite by pinpointing areas in your life where you notice positive conflict against the belief, and then repeat with emotion. This will make more sense shortly.

An anxious-preoccupied attachment style typically has the following core beliefs: I am abandoned, I am rejected, I am unheard, I am unimportant, I am excluded, I am unsafe, I am not good enough, I am unwanted, I am disliked, I am unloved, I am disconnected.

1. Using the core wounds list in the guide chapter, write down each core belief you have. You may feel some more intensely than others, and you may feel the majority of them. That's okay.

<u>Example:</u> I am abandoned, I am not good enough, I am unwanted, I am unheard, I am excluded, I am disliked.

_____

_____

_____

_____

_____

_____

_____

_____

2. Now, find the opposite to each of these core wounds.

<u>Example:</u> I am abandoned would turn into I am connected. I am bad would turn into I am good. (It is important to not say "I am not bad" because our brain doesn't register this the way we intend. It will pick up on the word *bad* and negate the attempt at reprogramming. For instance, when you're up high and you keep telling yourself, "Don't look down. Don't look down." What are you thinking about? Looking down. If I told you to look up, you're more likely to think about what's above, not what's below).

_____

_____

_____

_____

_____

_____

_____

_____

_____

_____

3. For each core wound that you wrote down, find its opposite in each area of life (you can find these in the guide chapter as well). Make sure you're really trying to feel this and not just saying it. **Repetition and emotion are needed for this to be effective.** For each wound (feel free to choose just a few to get started and come back later to work on the others), find at least three places in each area of life (from our guide chapter) where you do feel liked or included, or whatever wounds you are working on. After doing this **each day for a month**, you will start seeing a shift in negativity toward yourself and your self-esteem as a whole.

Example: Using the I am not good enough core wound . . . In the physical area of my life, I am good enough because I brushed my teeth today. (Doesn't matter how small; just matters that you're finding places). Physically, I am good enough because I went to the gym today. Physically, I am good enough because I'm bettering my diet.

_____

_____

_____

_____

_____

_____

_____

_____

Exercise 2: Questioning Stories

When we don't have all the pieces of the puzzle, we can create our own piece, whether it's factual or not, and begin to believe it. If you call someone and they don't answer, you may find yourself thinking it's because they don't want to talk to you, they're mad at you, they don't like you anymore. But really, you can't know. They could be in a meeting, had a terrible day, or forgot their phone at home. The point is, without *knowing*, it's dangerous to *assume*. It causes us to personalize, which heightens our insecurities and causes us to react based on the story instead of the facts.

1. Think of a problem or something that recently triggered you.

   Example: Maria didn't call me back even though she said she would.

   _____

   _____

   _____

   _____

   _____

   _____

2. What did you make that event mean or what core wound did you feel?

   Example: Maria must not care about me if she doesn't want to talk to me or I'm not important enough for her to remember.

   _____

   _____

_____

_____

_____

_____

_____

3. Can you be absolutely positive that this is the truth?

   Example: No.

   _____

   _____

4. What are other reasons this may not be true? We may tend to make ourselves unreasonably suffer by giving into negative stories that we can't know are one hundred percent true.

   Example: Maria might have innocently forgotten because she has a lot going on today. She might have lost track of time. Her phone might have died.

   _____

   _____

   _____

   _____

   _____

   _____

   _____

   _____

   _____

5. What is some evidence against what you're making it mean?

    Example: I know Maria cares because she brought me soup when I was sick last week and volunteered to help me paint my living room.

    _____

    _____

    _____

    _____

    _____

    _____

    _____

    _____

6. What did you need in the moment that you felt triggered?

    Example: I needed to feel cared about and I needed reassurance.

    _____

    _____

    _____

    _____

    _____

    _____

    _____

    _____

7. How can you meet this need? Or is this something you can communicate about? (If someone close to you is never available to communicate in a healthy and safe way, it may not be the best relationship. No one is perfect, but both parties need to be open to one another).

Example: I can find ways to make myself cared for and important like running a hot bath, making myself a nice dinner. I can gently ask Maria if next time, she can text that she can't talk so I don't feel anxious about waiting.

_____

_____

_____

_____

_____

_____

_____

_____

_____

_____

_____

Exercise 3: Protest Behaviors and Coping Mechanisms

When triggered, our subconscious kicks in and tries what it knows to protect us. This protection comes in the form of protest behaviors, or coping mechanisms. When we act in the form of these behaviors, it is us trying to get needs met. However, this can have the opposite effect at times – take the anxious and avoidant cycle for instance; the avoidant will withdraw, causing the anxious to cling, which in turn causes the avoidant to withdraw more. It is important to find what need we are actually trying to get met and find a healthier way to do that.

1. What is a protest behavior/coping mechanism you use? Feel free to look at the list or write one(s) down not mentioned.

Example: When Thomas randomly takes space, I continuously call his phone until he answers.

_____

_____

_____

_____

_____

_____

2. What do you hope to accomplish by doing this?

Example: By calling him and getting a response, I feel safer and less in danger of him leaving me.

_____

_____

_____

_____

_____

_____

_____

_____

3. What do you fear will happen if you don't take this action?

Example: If I don't have constant contact with him, it gives him room to forget me, or maybe he isn't answering right away because he does want to leave me.

_____

_____

_____

_____

_____

_____

_____

_____

_____

4. Do you know this will happen if you don't use this protest behavior?

Example: No, I can't be certain.

_____

_____

5. What are healthy ways to challenge or express this instead?

<u>Example:</u> I can work on having a better relationship with myself and meeting my own needs. I can also ask Thomas to communicate when he needs more space, letting him know I want him to have time for himself, too, but without context, I become anxious, thinking the worst.

_____

_____

_____

_____

_____

_____

_____

_____

_____

_____

_____

Exercise 4: Expectations

There are certain things we expect others to do. Sometimes, we may expect too much, like for someone to always be available, that people should never have arguments, that everyone should like us, or expect people to mindread (to automatically know what we want without us saying it). At times, we expect others to meet our needs for us. This is a trap anxious preoccupied and anxious-leaning disorganized individuals can get stuck in. Not knowing how to meet one's own needs can lead to expecting others to meet them for us, and actually feeling as though others are the only ones that can meet them for us. By questioning whether our expectations are fair, we can save ourselves a lot of pain and suffering.

1. Think of one relationship. What is something you expected recently that left you disappointed?

Example: I told Shelly I wasn't very good at choosing outfits for job interviews and I had an interview the next day. I expected her to offer to help me, but she didn't.

_____

_____

_____

_____

_____

2. What was at the root of your expectation? What did you want or need?

Example: For Shelly to help me pick out an outfit that would be good for my job interview.

_____

_____

_____

_____

_____

_____

3. Is it fair to assume the other person *should* know or do this?

_____

_____

4. How could you have gotten your need met or how can you get it met better next time?

Example: I could have communicated more directly that I need help picking an outfit, then I could have asked Shelly to go shopping with me, or I could have sent her pictures of several outfits and asked which was best.

_____

_____

_____

_____

_____

_____

_____

_____

Exercise 5: Rethinking the Mind-Reading Expectation

Continuing from the fourth exercise, sometimes there is expectation for mind reading because we are afraid to voice our need in fear of rejection or because we think if the other person automatically knows, we must have a deep connection, and figure if they don't know what we want, they must not really care. When we use the word *should,* we're already adding judgment and negativity to the expectation. This can be dangerous ground that can also make the other person irritated or feel as though they aren't good enough. This is also why questioning our stories is incredibly important – and when done often, will become a skill done in real time.

1. Think of the last time you expected mind reading.

Example: The movie adaptation of my favorite book came out and Jason didn't offer to take me to see it in theaters.

_____

_____

_____

_____

_____

2. Is there a reason you expected mind reading? Is there a reason you feared communicating your need?

Example: Jason should know I'm excited to see that movie. If I have to say it, he must not really know me.

_____

_____

_____

_____

_____

_____

_____

3. What did you make your fear mean about you or which core wound does this fear trigger in you?

Example: That I'm misunderstood and unloved.

_____

_____

_____

_____

4. How can you challenge this fear?

Example: Jason remembers most of the little things about me and makes me breakfast every morning.

_____

_____

_____

_____

5. Do you see that by focusing on the negative possibility, pain was caused?

_____

_____

_____

_____

Exercise 6: Mending Wounds

Fixing core wounds (also known as limiting beliefs or core beliefs) has a huge impact in becoming secure. Working on them can greatly increase your self-esteem and aide your relationships.

1. What are your top five core wounds – the ones you feel the most?

Example: I am abandoned. I am excluded. I am rejected. I am disliked. I am unsafe.

_____

_____

_____

_____

_____

2. Choose one. Then come back and do the others. When do you feel this wound the most?

Example: I am excluded. When my old high school friends go out to lunch without me.

_____

_____

_____

_____

_____

_____

_____

_____

_____

_____

3. What is your need in these instances?

Example: Feeling a sense of connection, togetherness, socialization.

_____

_____

_____

_____

_____

_____

_____

_____

_____

4. How am I able to get this need met for myself?

Example: Ask the new neighbors if they'd like to get lunch sometimes.

_____

_____

_____

_____

_____

_____

_____

_____

_____

Exercise 7: Understanding Your Needs

When our needs are getting met, we feel a sense of peace. When they are not getting met, we will feel discomfort that comes from our subconscious trying to get that need met for us. Usually when we cross our own boundaries, or allow them to be crossed, we are also ignoring a need of ours. Think about a time you hadn't left the house in a couple days and you were going stir-crazy. Maybe you were needing connection, or socialization, or adventure. There are all sorts of needs an individual subconsciously wants to get met, but when we don't know what these needs are or what our top ones are, it can be very difficult to decipher what our emotions are trying to tell us we need. And when we don't have them met, or go awhile without having them met, we will feel out of sync, or even depressed or irritable. Remember, it is our duty to meet our needs, and not fall into the trap of expecting others to meet them for us.

1. Write down your specific needs.

   Example: (A list here to get you started – feel free to pick from here and to add others to your own list). Love, freedom, communication, clarity, certainty, uncertainty, affection, harmony, order, belonging, trust, support, cooperation, contribution, growth, meaning, joy, power, integrity, authenticity, effectiveness, play, touch, rest, security, learning, rest, honesty, celebration, purpose, efficiency, dignity, intimacy, consideration, mutuality, spontaneity, compassion, understanding, autonomy, acceptance, wholeness, peace, ease, interconnection, creativity, self-expression, appreciation, inspiration, hope, reassurance, choice, nurturing, health, movement, relaxation, companionship, respect, listening, empathy, exercise, privacy, to be seen and heard, friendship, community, space, consistency, challenge, skill, novelty, adventure, presence, simplicity, focus, accomplishment, confidence, discovery, warmth, caring, kindness, humor, beauty, structure, independence, gentleness, spirituality, bonding, pleasure, protection, sense of self, sharing, inclusion, responsibility, partnership, equality, significance.

_____

_____

_____

_____

_____

_____

_____

_____

_____

_____

_____

_____

_____

_____

2. Rank your needs from highest to lowest. (This might be a little tricky, and it is okay if some feel like they rank the same. We just want to get an idea of your highest needs).

Example: Love, spirituality, adventure, meaning, certainty, creativity.

_____

_____

_____

_____

_____

_____

_____

_____

_____

_____

_____

_____

3. Do you feel all these needs are currently being met? Is there one, or are there many, that need to be met more or better? Which ones?

Example: Love, adventure, meaning.

_____

_____

_____

_____

_____

_____

_____

4. How do you feel when these needs are not met?

Example: Alone, bored, like I don't matter or what I do doesn't matter.

_____

_____

_____

_____

_____

_____

_____

_____

5. What are some healthy strategies to meet these needs?

Example: Connect with someone I care about. Start the craft business I've been wanting to do. Go on a hike.

_____

_____

_____

_____

_____

_____

_____

_____

_____

_____

6. Is there something you can start today to meet these needs? What is it?

Example: Call a friend or family member. Make a business outline.

_____

_____

_____

_____

_____

_____

_____

Exercise 8: Ranking Your Six Human Needs

Tony Robbins gives us six needs every human has. They are Certainty, uncertainty, love and connection, significance, growth, and contribution. Refer to chapter 4 for a brief overview. By knowing how you rank these based off importance, you can learn more about yourself and your own needs. If significance is highly important to you, you might find you need more validation in your life.

1. Rank the six human needs according to your preference. (There is no wrong answer. This is how they apply to you).

   _____

   _____

   _____

   _____

   _____

   _____

   _____

2. Do you feel you're fulfilling these needs in the same order you've ranked them?

   Example: I ranked love and connection as my most important, but it's not getting much attention.

   _____

   _____

   _____

   _____

   _____

   _____

_____

_____

_____

_____

_____

3. If you think some needs can be met more, what are some strategies to do this?

<u>Example:</u> I can use my upcoming day off work to visit my family instead of staying home.

_____

_____

_____

_____

_____

_____

_____

_____

_____

_____

_____

_____

_____

Exercise 9: Abandoning the Self

Anxious-preoccupied individuals many times abandon themselves in different areas of their lives. This is a reason why they reach out to others in order to get needs met. Looking inwardly is a scary thing for them to do. They are not usually used to having a strong relationship to the self. Sometimes, they may project the abandonment of themselves on someone else. For instance, if an anxious-preoccupied sees a parent not paying attention to his or her child, the anxiously attached individual might feel anger toward the parent and say, "They're not paying attention to their kid. They're abandoning their child in this moment." This is a good time to wonder if the weight of anger and unfairness is partly from projecting. Perhaps the anxious individual is abandoning himself or herself as well.

1. Where is a place you abandon yourself in your life? Use the areas of life guide in chapter 3 if it helps.

Example: I abandon myself in my career by doubting my abilities and not going toward my goals. I abandon myself when I try getting all my needs met by others instead of through myself.

_____

_____

_____

_____

_____

_____

_____

_____

_____

2. What are some strategies to spend time with yourself? (Quality time is key here. Make sure the time you're spending with yourself is not only watching television or scrolling on your phone. Try activities like cooking with yourself, watching the sunset, journaling, drawing, going for a jog).

Example: I can walk on the beach with my thoughts. I can work on crafts a few times a week.

_____

_____

_____

_____

_____

_____

3. How can you be fair to yourself in the areas of life you're used to abandoning yourself in?

Example: I can take small steps toward my career goals, starting with positive talk toward myself. I can learn my top needs and create strategies to meet them myself.

_____

_____

_____

_____

_____

_____

_____

_____

Exercise 10: Meeting Your Own Needs

As mentioned before, anxious-preoccupied individuals can struggle with meeting their needs for themselves. It can feel safer to get needs met by others, sometimes thinking that they *can't* meet their own needs well. A major help in meeting your own needs is by knowing what they are (see exercises 7 and 8). By identifying them and creating strategies to meet them on your own can do a lot of healing. Of course we need other people for different things, but when we put the weight of all our needs on others, it becomes harmful to them and us.

1. Think of your daily life. Who are the people you spend most of it with? Now, are there any needs you place on them to meet for you?

Example: Peace. Acceptance. Adventure.

_____

_____

_____

_____

_____

_____

_____

_____

_____

_____

_____

_____

_____

_____

_____

2. Why do you think you get these needs met externally?

Example: Kelly always has something fun going on and knows how to have an enjoyable time, so I feel like we're on an adventure whenever we hang out. That's why I try to see her as much as possible. Peace and acceptance, because certain people make me feel safe and loved, and I don't know how to find these on my own.

_____

_____

_____

_____

_____

_____

_____

_____

_____

3. How can you meet these needs on your own?

Example: I can research activities to do around my town for adventure. I can practice self-acceptance and healing which will also bring peace.

_____

_____

_____

_____

_____

_____

_____

_____

_____

_____

_____

_____

_____

_____

_____

_____

4. Can you find a strength in meeting these needs on your own instead of getting others to meet them for you?

Example: I don't have to wait for Kelly to be able to feel adventurous. I don't have to go to others to feel acceptance and peace when I accept myself and begin healing.

_____

_____

_____

_____

_____

_____

_____

_____

_____

_____

Exercise 11: Self-Soothing

For anxious-preoccupied individuals, self-soothing may not come naturally and can take some time to learn. A lot of this has to do with being present with one's self – something also difficult for the anxiously attached person since it can feel unsafe and unfamiliar as they are used to soothing through other people. So, in order for this to come more naturally, it is important to sit with yourself, find the needs you need met, and make it a point to be present with yourself. At first, taking quality time for yourself may feel boring, selfish, or scary, but taking small steps like this will add up in time.

1. When an event or situation occurs, how does it make you feel?

Example: I feel sad, confused, scared, angry, and disappointed when I am ignored.

_____

_____

_____

_____

_____

_____

_____

2. What are some things you need in order to feel better?

Example: Communication, understanding, consistency, transparency.

_____

_____

_____

_____

_____

_____

_____

_____

3. What are some ways you can get these needs met?

<u>Example:</u> Asking to find middle ground for the appropriate amount of communication. Questioning my stories. Using the time to do something of quality rather than ruminate.

_____

_____

_____

_____

_____

_____

_____

_____

_____

Exercise 12: Challenging Triggers

Becoming triggered, causes certain reactions. By knowing *why* we react in the way that we do, we can change our reaction with consistency and time. We do not go straight from trigger to reaction. Due to a form of past trauma, the trigger makes us activate or deactivate (primarily activate for the anxious-preoccupied). It causes us to feel negatively, which leads us to thinking negative thoughts and feeling negative emotions. They, then, cause us to react. The reaction we have is our way of trying to get a need met and protect ourselves from what we are afraid of. By bringing negative subconscious thoughts and emotions to light, we can better control our conscious. Without knowing what these are, it is easy for the subconscious to take over and make us react with a survival response since the subconscious is more powerful than the conscious, taking on much more information in a given moment than our conscious.

1. Think of something that triggers you and write it down.

Example: My boss telling me I did a poor job.

_____

_____

_____

_____

_____

2. Which core wound(s) do you feel because of this?

Example: I am not good enough. I am stupid. I am rejected.

_____

_____

_____

_____

_____

_____

_____

3. What thoughts go through your mind when you feel each of these?

Example: Not good enough – "I shouldn't even be at this job," "I can't do anything right." Stupid – "Anyone can do a better job than me," "I can't believe I'm such an idiot." Rejected – "My boss probably wants to fire me."

_____

_____

_____

_____

_____

_____

_____

4. What emotions do you feel when you have these thoughts?

Example: Stress. Worry. Fear. Shame. Sadness. Hopelessness. Frustration. Insult. Offense. Embarrassment. Hurt. Discomfort.

_____

_____

_____

_____

_____

5. What action follows?

Example: I don't share any of my ideas. I drink. I binge-eat.

_____

_____

_____

_____

6. What need is getting met by doing this?

Example: Comfort. Safety.

_____

_____

_____

_____

7. What is a healthier way to get these needs met in order to have a more positive reaction rather than a negative one?

Example: Taking a warm bath. Journal. Pray. Snuggle up with a cozy blanket. For the job itself, asking my boss what could have been done better for future reference, and letting myself know I did my best with what I knew at the time.

_____

_____

_____

_____

_____

_____

Exercise 13: Respecting & Communicating Boundaries

Respect around boundaries, of ourselves and others, is extremely important for a secure life. When we do not have boundaries of our own, it is easy to assume others do not, either, leading us to cross boundaries of the people around us. Boundaries being crossed can result in resentment, discomfort, hurt, anger, and weakening of relationships. It can be necessary to communicate your boundaries to others, as boundaries can differ from person to person, and sometimes one may not know when they are crossing a boundary. This is one reason why it is important to know your own boundaries. An example of someone else crossing your boundary would be your mother borrowing money and not paying it back as agreed upon. This would violate a material boundary – involving an object or money. An example of crossing your own boundary would be a coworker asking you to cover their shift, and knowing you have a class presentation to prepare for, you still say yes. This would be a violation of a time boundary.

1. When a boundary has been overstepped, you may feel discomfort, anxiety, frustration, or hurt. Write down a time you had a boundary crossed – whether by yourself or by someone else.

Example: Kendrick brought Alex as a plus one to my gathering without telling me.

_____

_____

_____

_____

_____

_____

_____

_____

_____

_____

_____

2. How did this cross your boundaries?

Example: Alex and I don't get along and I feel I should have been asked prior.

_____

_____

_____

_____

_____

_____

3. What thoughts or feelings did you have when this happened?

Example: Why would Kendrick bring someone I don't get along with? I felt annoyed and anxious. It made me nervous to invite Kendrick to future gatherings.

_____

_____

_____

_____

_____

_____

_____

_____

4. What are strategies for respecting your boundaries in the future?

Example: I can tell people it's invite only or have them ask me prior to inviting anyone else. I can tell Kendrick that even though I respect he and Alex get along well, Alex and I do not, and I would appreciate if that would be respected as well.

_____

_____

_____

_____

_____

_____

_____

_____

_____

_____

_____

_____

_____

_____

_____

Part II.

Knowing where your fear in *not* placing a boundary comes from is important as well. This will help you to understand why you may feel safer without a boundary, and how to show yourself boundaries are good.

1. Think of a time when someone (or yourself) asked for something and you said *yes* (or *no*) when you did not actually want to.

Example: A coworker asking me to cover their shift when I had other plans.

_____

_____

_____

_____

_____

_____

2. How did you feel when you crossed your boundary, or allowed your boundary to be crossed?

Example: I had discomfort and was irritated with my coworker for a while. I was annoyed with myself, and was upset I missed out on my plans.

_____

_____

_____

_____

_____

_____

_____

_____

_____

_____

_____

3. What were you afraid would happen if you respected the boundary?

Example: I would feel rude and selfish, and like I would no longer be liked.

_____

_____

_____

_____

_____

_____

_____

_____

4. Can you think of how respecting the boundary could have been a good thing?

Example: I would have felt empowered to respect my boundaries. I would have kept my plans. I would not have resentment toward this coworker. Maybe my coworker would have been upset with me, but it would pass.

_____

_____

_____

_____

_____

_____

_____

_____

_____

Exercise 14: When Conflict Arises

Conflict can be an uncomfortable thing. Scary, even. Many times, conflict feels like this because of our perception of it instead of its reality. Conflict can actually strength relationships if it is navigated in a healthy manner. When an argument arises, it is easy to deactivate by shutting down and withdrawing, or to activate by shouting and threatening to leave. The person withdrawing may seem they're giving up and don't care, when really they may be trying to protect the relationship by taking some time in order to not say something they'll regret, or they might feel criticized and therefore be feeling shame and want to hide. The person threatening to leave may not want to leave at all, but wants to be pulled back to know the other person cares. Arguments are each party attempting to be heard, but instead of hearing the other person, we tend to want to get the other person to hear us, while being too concerned with our own point. Some people will stick to this even when you try to come at it in a healthy and mutual way – this is when you need to ask if something is healthy enough to work on. When each party chooses to listen to the other, realizing the issue isn't with the person but the situation, healthy compromises can be made, and instead of arguing through relationships, there can be healthy communication. *If there is abuse in any relationship, it is important to leave.*

1. Think of a recent disagreement. Start by creating a safe place (not criticizing) and add something you appreciate (by being truthful here, it strengthens the safety). When we feel safe, we listen better, opposed to feeling attacked and trying to defend ourselves – this is where communication turns into unhealthy arguments that go nowhere.

Example: Marcy, I'm not criticizing you and I appreciate how close we are as roommates.

_____

_____

_____

_____

_____

_____

_____

_____

2. Take a sentence to explain what happened and how it made you *feel* (can insert a core wound here). Try your best to stick to "I" statements instead of "you" as one denotes blame.

Example: When I come into my room to find my clothes missing, it violates a boundary of mine.

_____

_____

_____

_____

_____

_____

3. The next step is to add why you felt this way. By being vulnerable, you're more likely to be heard by the other person. Remember to hear the other person as well.

Example: Sometimes the outfit being borrowed is the one I planned on wearing for the day.

_____

_____

_____

_____

_____

_____

_____

_____

_____

_____

_____

_____

4. Tell what you needed instead.

Example: I needed respect in this area.

_____

_____

_____

_____

_____

_____

_____

_____

_____

_____

_____

_____

5. How can this be given. Be as exact as you can. (One person might equate showing love by going out to dinner, while the person really wanted help cleaning the house).

Example: I needed respect by being asked first before borrowing an outfit. I love sharing my clothes with you, but I would appreciate the communication first.

_____

_____

_____

_____

_____

_____

_____

_____

_____

_____

_____

Continued:

After this, be ready and willing to listen to the other person, or even ask, "Does this make sense? Is there anything you would like to add?" This way, the other person knows what they have to share is important, too. Let the other person know you're hearing them and want to find compromise. Remember, be honest with this – don't find compromise by crossing your boundaries or agree to something you can't do. Respect for them and yourself.

Exercise 15: When Conflict Arises Pt. 2

In this exercise, you will learn how to open up a conversation when you feel someone may be hurt by something you did – whether directly or indirectly. This can also be a reply to someone coming to you with a problem in your relationship.

1. Let the person you're communicating with know you hear them, even by saying that exactly, "I hear you," and repeating what they've told you or if you're bringing it up, what you've noticed.

Example: I can see you may have felt powerless and excluded . . .

_____

_____

_____

_____

_____

_____

_____

2. Let them know you can understand why.

Example: . . . because I bought a sofa for our home without you.

_____

_____

_____

_____

_____

_____

_____

3. Insert how you felt.

Example: I felt rejected and unheard . . .

_____

_____

_____

_____

4. Add why.

Example: . . . because I had been looking forward to a new sofa for us since last year.

_____

_____

_____

_____

_____

_____

5. Find compromise.

Example: Can we find compromise together? If you don't like this sofa, we can return it and pick one out together.

_____

_____

_____

_____

_____

_____

Exercise 16: Communicating Love Languages

Knowing and communicating your love language and the love languages of those around you can help you to better receive and give love. It is normal to enjoy aspects of different love languages, but there will be those that stand out the most to you, maybe even one especially.

1. What makes you feel loved?

Example: When John does the dishes. When Margaret offers to watch the kids while John and I go on a date. When John carves out time for the date. When Sally and I have heart to hearts. When Margaret joins me to run errands. When John changes the car's oil.

_____

_____

_____

_____

_____

_____

_____

_____

_____

_____

_____

_____

_____

_____

_____

_____

_____

_____

_____

2. How do you show your love?

Example: Cooking dinner. Making thoughtful cards for friends just because. Doing crafts with the kids. Washing John's work truck. Having heart to hearts with Sally. Taking the kids back-to-school shopping.

_____

_____

_____

_____

_____

_____

_____

_____

_____

_____

_____

_____

_____

_____

3. Which love languages come up the most here?

Example: Quality Time and Acts of Service.

_____

_____

_____

_____

Exercise 17: Projected Positive Traits

When we become attached to people, we will find that many of their qualities and traits are ones that we either want in ourselves or we have repressed. We might not desire the traits we admire in the same area we see them in someone else, but want them in another area for ourself. An example is if one person is able to go out socializing and make friends with everyone there, we may want the traits of being outgoing and charming for the workplace, knowing it would help our confidence in meetings and success overall.

1. What are some traits you look for in a relationship, or even a friendship?

Example: Honesty, loyalty, enthusiasm, optimism, kindness, courage.

_____

_____

_____

_____

_____

_____

2. Do you have these traits yourself? Do you want any of these traits in yourself?

Example: I want more optimism, enthusiasm, and courage.

_____

_____

_____

_____

_____

3. How can you work on these traits for yourself?

Example: I can start a gratitude journal, be my own cheerleader, apply for that internship I've been nervous about.

_____

_____

_____

_____

_____

_____

_____

_____

4. What are some negative traits you have that challenge these?

Example: Pessimism. Dull. Fearful.

_____

_____

_____

_____

_____

5. Why do you have these in yourself, or why do they make you feel safe?

Example: I can't be let down if I expect the worst.

_____

_____

_____

_____

_____

6. How does holding onto these hold you back?

<u>Example:</u> I don't go after things I want. I don't speak up. I'm less confident.

_____

_____

_____

_____

_____

_____

_____

7. How can you let these go?

<u>Example:</u> Look for the positive side of things. Hope for the best. Realize failure happens, but it doesn't have to be the final result.

_____

_____

_____

_____

_____

_____

_____

_____

_____

Exercise 18: Seeing It Through Someone Else's Eyes

Many times, anxious-preoccupied individuals find themselves taking things personally, whether they were meant to or not. This can be excruciating at times, feeding into the negative beliefs they already have. Like questioning our stories, it is helpful to look through the other lens, trying to see where someone may have been coming from, rather than automatically taking it personally.

1. Think of a situation in which something was done that you took personally.

Example: Chloe canceled on me to go on a date with her new boyfriend.

_____

_____

_____

_____

_____

_____

2. Why might this person have done or said this? Can you find their innocence?

Example: She's been out of a relationship for a while and seems to really like this guy. It's new and exciting.

_____

_____

_____

_____

_____

_____

3. Is there any way this ended up being beneficial?

Example: My parents came over during the time I would have been spending with her and I got to spend some much-needed time with them.

_____

_____

_____

_____

_____

_____

_____

_____

_____

Exercise 19: Expectations and Others

In our relationships, things are so much easier when we are on the same page, try to understand each other, and communicate in a healthy way. Compromise, finding that middle ground, is an important piece of that. In order to get there, we need to know what our expectations are in the relationship, whether romantic or platonic, and what the other person's expectations are. Then, we can find common ground.

1. Think of a relationship in your life. What do you expect in this relationship? (Think of a certain situation if it helps).

Example: To see each other four times a week. Go to my parents for holidays. Go to a warm vacation destination outside the country.

_____

_____

_____

_____

_____

_____

_____

_____

_____

2. What do they expect in this relationship? (Ask them or try to gauge based on what they've told you so far).

Example: To see each other two times a week. Go to their parents for holidays. Go on vacation, but stay in the country.

_____

_____

_____

_____

_____

_____

_____

_____

_____

3. What is a healthy compromise here, being fair to both parties?

<u>Example:</u> To see each other three times a week. Split up holiday time spent at parents so we get to see both. Go on vacation to a warm destination inside the country.

_____

_____

_____

_____

_____

_____

_____

_____

_____

_____

_____

_____

Exercise 20: Turning Off Auto-Pilot

When we are hurting or trying to ease suffering, sometimes, we can fall into the trap of turning on our auto-pilot. We take up certain activities that are meant simply to waste time or make us temporarily feel better without having any lasting positive effects. By understanding what these are, when we do them, and *why* we do them, we can take back control. While some activities are harmful, there are those that are not *bad*, however can be used as a crutch to constantly distract us from what is going on around us and inside of us.

1. When I feel _____, I _____.

Example: When I am hurt, I play video games nonstop. When I feel alone, I binge television shows.

_____

_____

_____

_____

_____

_____

_____

_____

_____

2. What are you trying to accomplish by doing this?

Example: Distract myself. Escape. Find connection of some sort.

_____

_____

_____

_____

_____

_____

_____

_____

_____

_____

_____

_____

3. What are better ways to do this? Or what is a better response?

Example: Take a moment with myself to find out why I am hurt and investigate positive ways to help myself heal. Reach out to someone or connect with myself.

_____

_____

_____

_____

_____

_____

_____

_____

_____

_____

_____

_____

Exercise 21: Speaking to Your Inner Child

There will be times when we become afraid, like a child. We may even react similarly to a child in the attempt to get a need met. In times like these, we can talk to ourselves gently as we would a child. Instead of talking down to ourselves or feeding our mind more negativity and overflowing blame, we can calm ourselves and be patient and understanding as we would with a child – or even someone we care about.

1. What is a recent situation you were hard on yourself for?

Example: When I failed my exam.

_____

_____

_____

_____

2. If a child came to you about the same thing, how would you react toward the child?

Example: I would let the child know it is okay to fail sometimes – that it will happen from time to time. That they can't expect to be perfect, and to just try to do better next time. Then I would see if there was anything that would cheer them up.

_____

_____

_____

_____

_____

3. Can you give yourself the same courtesy?

_____

Exercise 22: Challenge Fears in a Relationship

When we are hurt in a relationship, whether heartbreak, disappointment from a friend or family member, trauma, or whatever it may be, we tend to carry the resulting fears with us into the next relationships. Subconsciously, we are being told it's to protect us, and we start to believe it is. But it can be incredibly damaging to those new relationships before they're given a chance. This can hurt you and the people around you. It's not your fault that this happens, but it is your responsibility. Pinpointing your fears can help you understand how to challenge them and have a healthier mindset behind new relationships.

1. What are my fears in a relationship? (You can think specific relationships or relationships in general; romantic or platonic).

Example: I'm afraid my friends will grow tired of me and leave me.

_____

_____

_____

_____

2. Where does this fear come from? (This is important to know because you may be able to find some core wounds within your answer, and work on those using exercise 1).

Example: My best friend started spending time with a new group, and stopped hanging out with me.

_____

_____

_____

_____

_____

3. Are my fears realistic in this/these current relationship(s)? Are they something I've carried with me?

<u>Example:</u> No, they are not realistic, and yes, I've carried them with me.

_____

_____

_____

4. What do I need to replace these fears with?

<u>Example:</u> Compassion for myself. Giving my new friends a chance.

_____

_____

_____

_____

5. How can I do this?

<u>Example:</u> Not expecting them to let me down by having faith in them. Understand that days they can't talk or don't want to hang out isn't because they're bored of me or will abandon me. Realize I have many traits of being a good friend.

_____

_____

_____

_____

_____

Final Note

Healing core beliefs and correcting negative responses can be a difficult journey, but one extremely beneficial. It will take time and effort on your part. It will also be one of the most worthwhile things you do. Consistency is key with any type of success. By doing these exercises when a specific issue arises, or other worksheets you find helpful, will drastically improve your self-worth, your ability to communicate healthier, your self-talk, as well as time management and self-esteem and confidence. Don't worry if you have bad days, even while working on yourself. This isn't a heal-all. You're going to have good days and bad days, but I genuinely hope this workbook will help you have more good days and a better outlook on yourself and others.

Remember: Love isn't only something you get. It's also something you give.

Share Love ♥

Access the **free downloadable PDF,** *Attachment Breakthrough Guide and Worksheets Crash Course* by going to https://bit.ly/join-tgt or use your phone to scan the code below.

Take the **Attachment Quiz** by going to https://bit.ly/takequiztgt or use your phone to scan the code below.

Check out **more books** from The Growth Tutorial by going to https://amzn.to/3TFEstk or use your phone to scan the code below.

Made in the USA
Monee, IL
30 October 2024

68997156R00056